The Debtor's Self-Help Guide
by Leroy Nibbs

The Debtor's Self-Help Guide
by Leroy Nibbs

© 2015 Leroy Nibbs

Published by www.debtorselfhelp.com

ISBN: 978-1-105-95119-0

Cover design by www.BigAppleWebDevelopers.com

Second Edition

Table of Contents

THE COLLECTION PROCESS 101 .... **1**

CHAPTER 1: REQUEST FOR DEPT VERIFICATION **7**
   TELEPHONE CALLS FROM COLLECTION AGENCIES ... 7
   RESPONDING TO COLLECTION LETTERS 8
   THE IMPORTANCE OF A REQUEST FOR DEBT VERIFICATION 9
      Sample Request for Debt Verification *12*
      Follow-Up Request for Debt Verification *13*
   THE DOWNSIDE OF MERELY TELLING A COLLECTOR TO STOP CALLING 15

CHAPTER 2: ACTING AS YOUR OWN LAWYER **17**
   RESPONDING TO A COMPLAINT AGAINST YOU 17
   SAMPLE ANSWER TO COMPLAINT 20
   SAMPLE MEMORANDUM OF LAW 26
   SAMPLE AFFIDAVIT IN SUPPORT OF ORDER TO SHOW CAUSE 36

CHAPTER 3: STATUTES OF LIMITATIONS .. **44**

GLOSSARY OF TERMS **45**

RECOMMENDED LEGAL RESOURCES **47**

TABLE OF CASES **48**

JUDICIAL DIVISIONS OF THE U.S. **51**

Disclaimer

DISCLAIMER: THE INFORMATION CONTAINED IN THIS BOOK IS PROVIDED FOR GENERAL INFORMATION ONLY. THE AUTHOR MAKES NO WARRANTY REGARDING THE ACCURACY OF THIS INFORMATION. WHILE SOME OF THE INFORMATION IS ABOUT LEGAL ISSUES, IT IS NOT LEGAL ADVICE. LEGAL QUESTIONS INVOLVING SPECIFIC LEGAL ISSUES SHOULD BE ADDRESSED TO AN ATTORNEY.

Introduction

The Debtor's Self-Help Guide is the only pro-debtor book that offers guidance and resources for an effective defense against unscrupulous collection agencies. The book contains practical and tested information and documents that help to keep debt collectors at bay.

Debt collectors rely on a consumer's lack of knowledge of the law and the legal process to intimidate the consumer and to take control of the debt collection process.

A fundamental understanding of the law and the legal process, as it relates to debt collection, will help you to achieve the best possible outcome. This book will teach you the fundamentals of debtor/creditor law and give you the tools to level the playing field.

The Collection Process 101

The collection process, which is a legal process, usually begins with a demand letter. In essence, a demand letter is a formal request for payment of an alleged debt. The letter must contain the name of the original creditor, the amount owed, and a notice of your right to dispute the debt.

> A **demand letter** or **dunning letter** is a letter that demands payment for an alleged debt. Collection agencies mail this letter to initiate the collection process.

If you do not respond to the demand letter, the collection calls begin. At this point, the debt collector assumes that the alleged debt is valid.

> **Never ignore a demand letter** from a collection agency, and always respond in writing. Chapter 1 contains a sample of an effective response.

If the collection process escalates, the collection agency will file a complaint against you. The complaint is the document filed with a court by a plaintiff to initiate a lawsuit against a defendant (the person being sued). The likelihood of the collection process escalating to this stage depends

The Collection Process 101

on a number of factors; however, since debt collectors prefer easy targets, an effective response to the demand letter certainly deters a debt collector from moving forward.

If a debt collector files a complaint against you, in addition to appearing on your court date, you should immediately file an answer with the court. There is a sample answer to a complaint in Chapter 2.

Before you respond to the complaint, keep in mind that the court is only concerned with substantive arguments that directly defend against the claims made by your opponent.

> **Substantive arguments** are arguments that are sufficiently important to require careful consideration by a court.

Let us assume that you could no longer pay the minimum payments on one of your credit cards, and you wanted to avoid accumulating late fees on that account. You therefore requested that ABC Credit Card Company close your account in May 2012, but ABC Credit Card Company refused to close your account, insisting that you must pay the entire balance before closing the account. Two years later, after 24 months of late fees had accumulated, ABC Credit Card Company files a lawsuit against you, claiming that you owe the amount that was due when you requested to have the account closed, plus 24 months of late fees.

> Take a minute to understand the definition of the word "**citation**" that we use in the next paragraph. A **citation** is a reference to case law, which a lower court in the same jurisdiction must follow, and other courts may find persuasive. We also use citations to refer to statutes (laws) or other legal authorities. Example of a case citation: *Cavallaro v. The Law Office of Shapiro & Krcsiman*, 933 F. Supp. 1148, 1153 (E.D.N.Y. 1996).

In your response to the court (your answer), you would explain the above facts, and add the following case opinions and citations from our sample documents to strengthen your argument:

A significant portion of plaintiff's alleged "damages" are self-incurred, and "self-incurred damages are not recoverable under the doctrine of avoidable consequences." *Jenkins v. Graham*, 237 So..2d 330, 332 (Fla. Dist. Ct. App. 1970).

Further, Plaintiff failed to mitigate their damages and therefore, "… cannot get judgment for the amount of this avoidable and unnecessary

The Collection Process 101

increase." Restatement, Contracts, § 336, subd [1], *Manufacturers & Traders Trust Co. v. Holley*, 438 N.Y.S.2d. 676, 688 (N.Y. City Ct. 1981).

Moreover, in *Cohen v. Banks*, 642 N.Y.S.2d 797, 802 (1996), the Court ruled that the Plaintiff could not recover for injuries she might have reasonably avoided by timely prudent action because of the Plaintiff's "determination to maximize them (damages) rather than seeking legal relief."

> **Caselaw** or **case law** is **law created by decisions in earlier court cases**, which a lower court within a given jurisdiction must follow, and other courts often find persuasive.

Chapter 2 explains more about responding to a complaint. For now, keep in mind that judges do not arbitrarily decide cases. There are clearly defined rules in our court system. Among these rules is the requirement that **all judges in a given jurisdiction follow case law from higher courts in that jurisdiction**.

Given this requirement, it is always helpful to support your arguments with quotes from pro-debtor decisions in earlier cases. Good case citations undoubtedly give weight to your statements and may ultimately help you to persuade the judge and win.

The Collection Process 101

Citations are also effective to contradict your opponent's position. See pages 38 through 42 for an excellent example.

Absent the use of case law, you would need to compose your own legal arguments. To the extent possible, you must make use of the pro-debtor decisions from earlier lawsuits.

As a final point, note that debt collectors want to collect all debts short of full-scale litigation, or in the less desirable alternative, to secure a collectable judgment against you for the amount owed. A judgment against you is basically a court order directing you to pay the amount owed.

The next step in the collection process is the enforcement of the judgment. Enforcement includes the right to garnish a portion of your salary, to serve restraining notices on banks with which you have an account (to freeze funds), and to place liens on your real property (house, land, etc.). If all else fails, the collector may seize or sell your non-exempt assets to satisfy the judgment.

In conclusion, the collection process is time-consuming and filled with potential liability for debt collectors at every stage. This means that debt collectors want to negotiate, partly to avoid the pitfalls of strict federal and state regulations. You should note that any mutual agreement or

The Collection Process 101

stipulation of settlement between you and the debt collector must be in writing and signed by both parties, preferably before a judge.

Also note that if the collection agency files a lawsuit and you reach a settlement before the matter goes to trial, you would use a stipulation of settlement to document the terms of your settlement. Both parties sign the stipulation and the court keeps a copy on file. To make certain that the stipulation permanently concludes the matter, you must ensure that the stipulation contains a statement dismissing the matter **with prejudice**.

Chapter 1: Request for Debt Verification

After completing this chapter, you will:

- ✓ Know how to respond to telephone calls from collection agencies
- ✓ Know how to respond to collection letters
- ✓ Understand the importance of a request for debt verification

Telephone Calls from Collection Agencies

The Fair Debt Collection Practices Act ("FDCPA") is the law that spells out what **debt collectors** can and cannot do in their efforts to collect debts. This law gives you, the person who owes money (the debtor), specific rights and recourse if a collection agency violates those rights.

The FDCPA states that a collection agency must notify you of your right to dispute a debt within five (5) days of the collection agency's initial communication with you. The FDCPA calls the notice required of the debt collector a "validation notice." In essence, the written validation notice tells you, the debtor, that you have thirty days (30)

Chapter 1: Request for Debt Verification

within which to dispute the debt, or the collection agency will assume that the alleged debt is valid.

If a collection agency starts the collection process by telephoning you, you should request a demand letter, and terminate the call. In other words, if a debt collector calls you with a claim that you owe money to ABC Company, you should request written communication and terminate the call. You should not say another word. Just say, "Put it in writing."

Responding to Collection Letters

Congress named the Fair Debt Collection Practices Act (FDCPA), 15 U.S.C. § 1692g, "validation of debts," and the response required of the debt collector pursuant to this section, "debt verification." A request for debt verification is a written request to a debt collector from a debtor to provide specific information to establish that you (the debtor) owe money. You use a request for debt verification letter to dispute a debt. The letter stops the collection process until the debt collector sends you proof that you owe money.

You MUST respond to letters from collection agencies or demand letters with a request for debt verification. The law requires that you respond within thirty days (30) after you receive a written

Chapter 1: Request for Debt Verification

communication from the collection agency, which contains a statement notifying you that you have thirty days to dispute the debt (the "validation notice").

The Importance of a Request for Debt Verification

> Always mail documents that you could possibly need as evidence in court via CERTIFIED MAIL, RETURN RECEIPT REQUESTED, unless otherwise instructed by a judge.

Part of the effectiveness of a request for debt verification comes from the mystery surrounding the statutory requirements to fulfill a request. In other words, a number of collection agencies simply do not know how to satisfy a request for debt verification. Additionally, the requirements are not static, since case law, which varies by jurisdiction (circuits), can modify the requirements at any time. Moreover, debt collectors often do not have access to the information required to satisfy a request for debt verification, or they find the process too burdensome. Also note that the FDCPA is a strict liability statute (see *Russell v. Equifax A.R.S.*, 74 F.3d 30, 33 [2d Cir. 1996]) and any act that violates the regulations of the FDCPA gives rise to liability, regardless of whether the

Chapter 1: Request for Debt Verification

consumer suffered any actual damage as a result. Further, "...a single violation of the Act is sufficient to impose liability." See *Cavallaro v. The Law Office of Shapiro & Kresiman*, 933 F. Supp. 1148, 1153 (E.D.N.Y. 1996) citing *Bentley v. Great Lakes Collection Bureau*, 6 F.3d 60, 62 (2d Cir.1993).

A request for debt verification tells a debt collector that you are well informed. Keep in mind that debt collectors are far more likely to abuse or otherwise take advantage of you, if they believe you are uninformed. In addition, verification not only ensures that the amount claimed is accurate; it **also helps to verify that the collector has the authority to collect the debt and act as agent for the original creditor**. A good request for debt verification capitalizes on the mystery surrounding the statutory requirements of satisfying the request. Specifically, the language in an effective request does not tell the debt collector what would satisfy the debtor's request for verification. Also take into account that **any specific information requested by the debtor may not necessarily satisfy the requirements of the law**.

In summary, an effective request for debt verification:

1. **Helps to verify that a collection agency has the authority to collect a debt;**

Chapter 1: Request for Debt Verification

2. Immediately stops all communication with you;

3. **Demands proof of indebtedness from a collection agency and uncovers hidden fees and other charges**;

4. Halts any plan to sue you;

5. Puts you in control of the collection process;

6. Earns you the respect needed to negotiate a fair settlement;

7. **Stops collectors from reporting to credit reporting agencies***;

8. Does not adversely affect your credit score;

9. Compels some collection agencies to abandon collection efforts; and

10. Gives you time to get on your feet.

*See the Fair Credit Reporting Act ("FCRA"), 15 U.S.C. § 1681(i), 15 USCS § 1681s-2 and FTC Staff Opinion Letter, 1997 WL 33791232 (F.T.C.) (Dec. 23, 1997)

Chapter 1: Request for Debt Verification

Sample Request for Debt Verification

> The following is an effective request for debt verification letter:

RE: Your acct. №:

To Whom It May Concern:

Please take notice that I hereby dispute the subject debt in its entirety, and I request detailed and sufficient verification in accordance with 15 USCS § 1692 et seq. and applicable case law.

Additionally, please provide an itemized statement of all charges, fees, and any other amounts that are a part of the alleged debt, together with all evidence of indebtedness in the original creditor's possession.

Best regards,
Your Name

Chapter 1: Request for Debt Verification

Sample Follow-up Request for Debt Verification

If the collection agency's response to your request for debt verification does not satisfy you, follow up with the second request for debt verification.

> Here is an effective follow-up request for debt verification letter:

RE: Second request for debt verification
      Your account №:

To Whom It May Concern:

Despite my request for verification of the subject debt, you have refused to provide verification, and continue collection efforts in violation of 15 USCS § 1692 et seq.

With reference to your communication dated October 8, the generic document you included as verification of the alleged debt falls far short of the precedential standard of verification in the 2nd circuit, and therefore fails to verify the alleged debt.

Chapter 1: Request for Debt Verification

Again, I hereby dispute the subject debt in its entirety, I and request detailed and sufficient verification in accordance with 15 USCS § 1692 et seq. and applicable case law.

Best regards,
Your Name

> Replace "**2nd Circuit**" with the corresponding circuit for your state. See pages 51 to 54.

Chapter 1: Request for Debt Verification

The Downside of Merely Telling a Collector to Stop Calling

The Fair Debt Collection Practices Act (FDCPA) of 1978 is a federal statute that protects consumers from abusive creditors/collection agencies and provides an effective means to dispute or verify the validity of a debt.

The following applicable subsection of the FDCPA (15 USCS § 1692c[c]) stops harassing communications; however, it does not preclude a collection agency from filing a lawsuit against you:

§ 1692c. Communication in connection with debt collection
(c) Ceasing communication. If a consumer notifies a debt collector in writing that the consumer refuses to pay a debt or that the consumer wishes the debt collector to cease further communication with the consumer, the debt collector shall not communicate further with the consumer with respect to such debt, except--
(1) to advise the consumer that the debt collector's further efforts are being terminated;
(2) to notify the consumer that the debt collector or creditor may invoke specified remedies which are ordinarily invoked by such debt collector or creditor; or
(3) where applicable, to notify the consumer that the debt collector or creditor intends to invoke a

Chapter 1: Request for Debt Verification

specified remedy. If such notice from the consumer is made by mail, notification shall be complete upon receipt.

This alternative to ending communication from a debt collector (merely requesting that a debt collector cease communication) leaves the debt collector's hands untied, and the debt collector can continue collection activity by filing a lawsuit against you.

In short, a request for debt verification is much more effective, since there are numerous benefits and zero consequences.

In fact, some debt collectors simply abandon collection efforts after they receive a request for debt verification. If the current collection agency abandons collection efforts, a new collection agency may begin collection activity. Note that the collection process restarts when a new debt collector contacts you. **This means that you must make a new request for debt verification with each new collection agency.**

> The **FDCPA protects consumers** from unethical collection practices, regardless of whether a debt actually exists.

Chapter 2: Acting As Your Own Lawyer

Chapter 2: Acting As Your Own Lawyer

After completing this chapter, you will:

- ✓ Know how to respond to a complaint against you
- ✓ Know how to vacate a default judgment against you
- ✓ Know how to deal with a collection agency that ignored your request for debt verification and continued collection activity

Responding to a Complaint Against You

If you receive a complaint against you, you should file an answer to the complaint, especially when you plan to represent yourself. The answer gives you an opportunity to carefully shape your argument on paper and provide supporting citations to persuade the judge. This is your opportunity to present a written cogent argument to the judge within the prescribed time.

A memorandum of law (or a legal brief) is a more expansive pleading that builds on your answer or other pleadings by providing the court with your detailed arguments and supporting citations,

Chapter 2: Acting As Your Own Lawyer

including case law, which lower courts must follow, and other courts may find persuasive.

> Note that **case law** is **law created by decisions in earlier court cases**, which lower courts within a given jurisdiction must follow, and other courts often find persuasive.

If the pleadings that you submit to the court before your court date are effective and your matter goes to trial, there is a good chance that you may prevail before you even set foot in court. Alternatively, **if you do not respond, the experienced lawyer gets the only opportunity to influence the court before your court date.**

In short, you must challenge the substance of your opponent's complaint, and respond to each allegation (respond with an affirmative defense [an opposing assertion] if one is available). Even if your matter does not go to trial, effective pleadings may force the opposing party to the negotiating table. Effective pleadings tell your opponent that you are a formidable adversary. Regardless of the facts of your case, all collectors want the easy and less costly alternative to resolving issues.

Chapter 2: Acting As Your Own Lawyer

> Respond to each allegation with one of the following: 1. *Admit*, 2. *Deny*, 3. *Upon information and belief, Deny*, or 4. *Deny knowledge or information sufficient to form a belief.*

The following documents are an Answer and a Memorandum of Law to a complaint against a debtor for an alleged credit card debt. Please use the promotional code **BOOK1** to save 50% on the Microsoft Word version of these and other documents from www.debtorselfhelp.com.

Keep in mind that debt collectors use legal documents to start and end the collection process. Your best defense is the use of effective and opposing legal documents to bring about an outcome in your favor. Note that you can modify all of the sample documents in this book to fit your unique set of circumstances. Simply state the facts of your case, and then search the sample documents for on-point quotes and citations. All of the citations are real references to cases or other legal authorities. Please use them to your advantage.

Chapter 2: Acting As Your Own Lawyer

Sample Answer to Complaint

CIVIL COURT OF THE CITY OF NEW YORK
COUNTY OF KINGS

CREDITOR'S NAME, Plaintiff,	Index No.: 00000-09
vs.	**ANSWER AND COUNTERCLAIM**
YOUR NAME, Defendant.	

Defendant, Your Name, pro se, as and for his answer to the complaint of Plaintiff, ABC Credit Card Company, states as follows:

1. Defendant, Your Name, admits the allegation of the complaint set forth in paragraph "2" (That Defendant resides in the county in which action is brought) of the complaint.

2. Defendant denies the allegations of the complaint set forth in paragraphs "1," "3," "4," "5," "6," and "7" of the complaint.

Chapter 2: Acting As Your Own Lawyer

AS AND FOR A FIRST AFFIRMATIVE DEFENSE

3. Defendant received an unsolicited letter from the Creditors Name (hereinafter "CN") stating that Defendant was "pre-approved" to receive a secured credit card provided that Defendant (a) had income of at least $1,000.00 per month and (b) would deposit at least $200.00 in a savings account with CN. The application required an additional application fee of $50. Defendant's first billing statement is annexed hereto and made a part hereof as, "Exhibit A."

4. Prior to receiving CN's offer for a secured credit card, Defendant had never solicited or received credit from any creditor, and as such, never had a credit history. For this reason, Defendant was unsuccessful in benefiting from the conveniences of a credit card from a well-thought-of lender.

5. Unaware of CN's history of deceptive business practices (See annexed FTC cases against and involving Plaintiff [*FTC v. American Standard Credit Sys.*, 874 F. Supp. 1080 and FTC v. US Sales Corp., 785 F. Supp. 737]), Defendant responded with the application and a U.S. Postal Money Order for Two Hundred Dollars ($200.) and subsequently received a cash-secured credit card with a Two Hundred Dollar Sixty Dollar ($260.)

Chapter 2: Acting As Your Own Lawyer

credit limit, which was equal to the amount deposited in Defendant's savings account with CN plus Sixty Dollars ($60.). However, the available credit was Two Dollars ($2.). See "Exhibit A."

6. Accordingly, Plaintiff owes Defendant the said Two Hundred Dollar ($200.) initial savings deposit together with interest thereon as promised.

AS AND FOR A SECOND AFFIRMATIVE DEFENSE

7. Defendant repeats and realleges the allegations contained in Paragraphs 3 through 6 with the same force and effect as if fully set forth herein.

8. Consistent with the deceptive practices that resulted in the FTC's action against Plaintiff, this issue is the outcome of Plaintiff's adamant refusal to waive late and resulting over-limit fees when Defendant made his monthly payment on the payment due date (via MoneyGram), after Plaintiff's unpublished 3:00 P.M. cutoff time for same-day posting to Defendant's account. Despite Plaintiff's immediate receipt of Defendant's electronic payment, Plaintiff subsequently charged Defendant a late fee, which caused Defendant's balance to exceed the abovementioned credit limit, after which Plaintiff

Chapter 2: Acting As Your Own Lawyer

charged Defendant an over-limit fee, together with substantial interest thereon. Plaintiff applied these fees and interest to Defendant's account for several months after Defendant requested that Plaintiff close the account, and Defendant discontinued using the subject credit card.
For the foregoing reasons, a significant portion of plaintiff's alleged "damages" are self-incurred, and "self-incurred damages are not recoverable under the doctrine of avoidable consequences." *Jenkins v. Graham*, 237 So..2d 330, 332 (Fla. Dist. Ct. App. 1970).

AS AND FOR A THIRD AFFIRMATIVE DEFENSE

9. Defendant repeats and realleges the allegations contained in Paragraphs 3 through 6 with the same force and effect as if fully set forth herein.

10. "Generally the law frowns upon the secured party's retaining possession of security for an extended period of time. As an indication of this, § 9-505(1) of the Uniform Commercial Code requires that goods under certain conditions must be sold within 90 days." See *United States v. Pirnie*, 339 F. Supp. 702 (1972).

11. Further, it is clear that "most courts have found that a creditor who retains collateral for an unreasonably long time can be deemed to have

Chapter 2: Acting As Your Own Lawyer

retained the collateral in full satisfaction of its debt under § 9-505(2) of the Uniform Commercial Code, even though the creditor failed to comply with the notice requirement of the statute." See *Lamp Fair, Inc. v. Perez-Ortiz*, 888 F.2d 173, 176-77 (1st Cir. 1989) and *Millican v. Turner*, 503 So. 2d 289, 291 (Miss. 1987).

12. In the case at hand, CN has held and deprived the Defendant of his cash deposit for over three (3) years without any communication whatsoever. CN should therefore be deemed to have retained the collateral in full satisfaction of the debt under § 9-505(2) of the Uniform Commercial Code.

13. In keeping with § 9- 505(2) of the Uniform Commercial Code, where a creditor elects to retake the collateral and "keep it as his own", he shall be held to have discharged the obligation and abandoned any claim for a deficiency.

AS AND FOR A FOURTH AFFIRMATIVE DEFENSE

14. Plaintiff, in paragraph "5" of the complaint, alleges that, "The total balance under said agreement is $556.81 as of 04/23/04." In fact, the subject account that Defendant opened with Plaintiff had a secured credit limit of Two Hundred Sixty Dollars ($260.), and up to the date

Chapter 2: Acting As Your Own Lawyer

Defendant requested that Plaintiff close said account and Defendant discontinued using the credit card, neither Defendant nor any other person charged services or goods to exceed Defendant's Two Hundred Sixty Dollars ($260.) credit limit.

AS AND FOR A COUNTERCLAIM

15. Defendant repeats and realleges the allegations contained in Paragraphs 3 through 6 with the same force and effect as if fully set forth herein.

WHEREFORE, Defendant demands judgment against Plaintiff dismissing Plaintiff's complaint for prior satisfaction of debt pursuant to § 9-505(2) of the Uniform Commercial Code, or in the alternative, deduct Defendant's Two Hundred Dollar ($200) initial savings deposit plus interest thereon from any amount due Plaintiff, together with such other and further relief as this court may deem just and proper.

> **Note that your Answer can also include a cross-claim (a claim against a third-party to the lawsuit) against Plaintiff's attorney for violation of the FDCPA.**

Chapter 2: Acting As Your Own Lawyer

Sample Memorandum of Law

CIVIL COURT OF THE CITY OF NEW YORK
COUNTY OF KINGS

CREDITOR'S NAME, 　　　　　Plaintiff, 　　　vs. **YOUR NAME,** 　　　　　Defendant.	Index No.: 00000-09 **MEMORANDUM OF LAW IN SUPPORT OF DEFENDANT'S ANSWER, CROSS-CLAIM AND MOTION TO DISMISS PLAINTIFF'S COMPLAINT FOR VIOLATION OF THE FDCPA**

MEMORANDUM OF LAW

PRELIMINARY STATEMENT

This is an action brought by the plaintiff against defendant, seeking $2,028.84 plus interest and

Chapter 2: Acting As Your Own Lawyer

attorney fees for an alleged credit card debt. The claims stem from Plaintiff's adamant refusal to waive late and resulting over-limit fees when Defendant made his monthly payment on the payment due date (via MoneyGram), after Plaintiff's unpublished ~3:30 P.M. cutoff time for same-day posting to Defendant's account. Despite Plaintiff's immediate receipt of Defendant's electronic payment, Plaintiff subsequently charged Defendant late fees, which ultimately caused Defendant's balance to exceed his Five Hundred Dollar ($500) credit limit, after which Plaintiff added over-limit fees, together with substantial interest thereon. Plaintiff applied these fees and interest to Defendant's account for over a year after Defendant's written request to close the subject account, and Defendant had discontinued using the subject credit card.

INTRODUCTION

3. Congress named the Fair Debt Collection Practices Act (FDCPA) 15 U.S.C. § 1692g, "validation of debts," and the response required of the debt collector pursuant to this section, "debt verification."

4. 15 U.S.C. § 1692g requires a debt collector to send a consumer written notice ("validation notice") regarding the debt within five days of the initial communication between the debt collector

Chapter 2: Acting As Your Own Lawyer

and the consumer. The notice must contain statutorily specified information including:

(1) the amount of the debt;

(2) the name of the creditor to whom the debt is owed;

(3) a statement that unless the consumer, within thirty days after receipt of the notice, disputes the validity of the debt, or any portion thereof, the debt will be assumed to be valid by the debt collector;

(4) a statement that if the consumer notifies the debt collector in writing within the thirty-day period that the debt, or any portion thereof, is disputed, the debt collector will obtain verification of the debt or a copy of a judgment against the consumer and a copy of such verification or judgment will be mailed to the consumer by the debt collector; and

(5) a statement that, upon the consumer's written request within the thirty-day period, the debt collector will provide the consumer with the name and address of the original creditor, if different from the current creditor.

5. Black's Law Dictionary's 1548 (7th ed.1999) definitions of the key statutory terms (root words), "verification" and "validation," of the act are as follows:

Chapter 2: Acting As Your Own Lawyer

Verify: To prove to be true; to confirm or establish the truth or truthfulness of; to authenticate.

Valid: 1. Legally sufficient; binding.

6. Based on the foregoing, Congressional intent of the Fair Debt Collection Practices Act (FDCPA), 15 U.S.C. § 1692 et seq., was clearly to require debt collectors to provide evidentiary verification of a disputed debt, as no mention of verifying the debtor's identity or creditor's claim was made, and we cannot disregard "the strong presumption that Congress expresses its intent through the language it chooses." See *INS v. Cardoza-Fonseca*, 480 U.S. 421, 432 n.12, 94 L. Ed 434, 107 S. Ct. 1207 (1987).

PLAINTIFF'S ATTORNEY REFUSED TO PROVIDE THE MANDATORY FDCPA DEBT VERIFICATION

7. On February 17, 2007 Defendant requested debt verification (annexed as Exhibit A) in accordance with 15 U.S.C. § 1692 et seq.

8. On February 26, 2007 Plaintiff's attorney responded (annexed as Exhibit B) with previously provided information, except that the amount claimed conflicted with the initial demand, and no confirmation whatsoever.

Chapter 2: Acting As Your Own Lawyer

8b. "In providing that the consumer may obtain verification by disputing the debt within 30 days of receipt of the initial communication, the FDCPA clearly contemplates that the verification is separate and distinct from the initial communication." See *Anderson v. Frederick J. Hanna & Assocs.*, 361 F. Supp. 2d 1379 (2005).

9. There is no doubt that the experienced debt collectors and attorneys at Creditor's Name know exactly what "debt verification" is, and the response required to satisfy the requirements thereof. Further, there is no reference to enclosures or attachments in Plaintiff's attorney response to Defendant's request for "debt verification" to indicate an error or omission. For these reasons, we can reasonably conclude that Plaintiff's attorney willfully refused to provide the requisite verification. Moreover, considering that at least eighty (80) percent of the alleged debt consists of fees and exorbitant interest, it is no surprise that Plaintiff's attorney refused to provide the mandatory debt verification, since debt verification would have unveiled this fact.

10. Even if "Verification of a debt involves nothing more than the debt collector confirming in writing that the amount being demanded is what the creditor is claiming is owed," Plaintiff's attorney's February 26 letter contained no such confirmation.

Chapter 2: Acting As Your Own Lawyer

11. In any event, Plaintiff's attorney purported debt verification did not confirm that the amount being demanded is what creditor claims is owed, and the amount claimed in the supposed verification is higher than the amount claimed in the initial demand letter, and, therefore, does not confirm the amount Plaintiff claimed in their communications. The alleged debt verification and the initial demand letter are annexed hereto and made a part hereof as Exhibit B and C respectively.

12. Plaintiff's attorney's response to Defendant's request for debt verification fell short of the standard of verification in prevailing cases. In *Graziano v. Harrison*, 950 F.2d 107, 113 (3d Cir. 1991) creditor's attorneys provided "computer printouts ... sufficient to inform him (debtor) of the amounts of his debts, the services provided, and the dates on which the debts were incurred." See also *Bascom v. Dubin*, 2007 U.S. Dist. LEXIS 5349 (2007) where "The letter defendant provided to plaintiffs dated February 5, 2002 included copies of billing statements, which were generated prior to the charge off of the plaintiffs' account and an Affidavit of Claim and Certification of Amount Due from Stephanie Roland dated February 1, 2002 concerning the original debt and amount owed by plaintiffs, were sufficient to verify the debt. The account statement consisted of a computer print out that sufficiently informed

Chapter 2: Acting As Your Own Lawyer

plaintiffs that the amount being demanded is what the defendant is claiming is owed and showed the dates on which charges were incurred."

13. Accordingly, Plaintiff is barred from filing suit because Plaintiff's attorney failed to provide the requisite debt verification in accordance with the Fair Debt Collection Practices Act, 15 U.S.C. § 1692g(b). That section of the FDCPA provides that, if a consumer notifies a debt collector within 30 days of receipt of an initial communication regarding collection of a debt that the debt is disputed, the debt collector must "cease collection of the debt" until it "obtains verification of the debt or a copy of a judgment, or the name and address of the original creditor, and a copy of such verification or judgment, or name and address of the original creditor, is mailed to the consumer by the debt collector."

14. Plaintiff's attorney's failure to provide the requisite debt verification and Plaintiff's commencement of a lawsuit prior to providing the said debt verification is a violation of the Fair Debt Collection Practices Act, 15 U.S.C. § 1692g(b), as the lawsuit is undoubtedly "collection activity." See *Heintz v. Jenkins*, 514 U.S. 291 (1995) and *Anderson v. Frederick J. Hanna & Assocs.*, 361 F. Supp. 2d 1379 (2005).

Chapter 2: Acting As Your Own Lawyer

CONCLUSION

15. Plaintiff's attorney's commencement of a lawsuit prior to providing the mandatory debt verification is a violation of the Fair Debt Collection Practices Act's prohibition on continuing collection activity prior to providing debt verification, as Plaintiff's attorney was required to "cease collection of the debt" until it "obtains verification of the debt," 15 U.S.C. § 1692g(b), and "A single violation of the Act is sufficient to impose liability." See *Cavallaro*, 933 F.Supp. at 1153 (citing *Bentley v. Great Lakes Collection Bureau*, 6 F.3d 60, 62 [2d Cir.1993]).

WHEREFORE, Defendant demands judgment against Plaintiff dismissing complaint, and judgment against Plaintiff's attorneys, awarding the maximum $ 1,000.00 in statutory damages to Defendant pursuant to 15 U.S.C. §1692k(a), including actual damages, and additional damages as permitted by the Court, together with such other and further relief as this Court may deem just and proper.

DEMAND IS HEREBY MADE that Plaintiff's attorneys answer the cross-claims against it, contained herein, and that service of such answers be made upon the undersigned within twenty (20) days after service of this answer and cross-claim.

Chapter 2: Acting As Your Own Lawyer

> **Court rules vary by jurisdiction.** For example, New York requires that a person making a cross-claim (a claim against a third-party to a lawsuit) demand a response (an answer) or the cross-claim may be denied (See New York CPLR 3011).

> **Do not be discouraged by court rules.** You can always ask the court to follow cases like *Boissevain v. Boissevain*, 252 NY 178, 169 NE 130 (1929), "Where the appropriate remedy upon the facts alleged was different from the relief asked for in the pleading, case was remitted in order that appropriate relief might be granted on the facts and judgment dismissing the complaint was reversed." Also see *Pattison v. Pattison*, 301 NY 65, 92 NE2d 890 (1950), where the court concluded that "Mistake in remedy was not ground for dismissing complaint, as it could have been corrected under CPA § 111 (N.Y. Civ. Prac. Act § 111)."

Chapter 2: Acting As Your Own Lawyer

> Pursuant to New York CPLR § 3017 and CPLR § 2001 respectively, a court "...may grant any type of relief within its jurisdiction appropriate to the proof whether or not demanded, imposing such terms as may be just," or "At any stage of an action, the court may permit a mistake, omission, defect or irregularity to be corrected, upon such terms as may be just, or, if a substantial right of a party is not prejudiced, the mistake, omission, defect or irregularity shall be disregarded." See *Sager v. Sager*, 21 A.D.2d 183, 249 N.Y.S.2d 467 (3d Dep't 1964). See also N.Y. Civ. Prac. Act § 111 which "makes it the duty of any court at any time in the state to disregard a mistaken prayer for relief and all formal defects in a pleading before or after judgment, and to administer the proper relief if it has jurisdiction on any statements of facts properly pleaded and proved."

The foregoing Memorandum of Law accompanies the shorter Motion to Dismiss.

Chapter 2: Acting As Your Own Lawyer

> Use an **Order to Show Cause** to vacate a default judgment against you. When the court vacates a default judgment, it simultaneously vacates all restraining notices on file with your banks and ends salary garnishments.

Sample Affidavit in Support of Order to Show Cause

CIVIL COURT OF THE CITY OF NEW YORK
COUNTY OF KINGS

CREDITOR'S NAME, Plaintiff,	Index No.: 00000-09
vs. **YOUR NAME,** Defendant.	**AFFIDAVIT IN SUPPORT OF ORDER TO SHOW CAUSE** To Vacate a Judgment and to Restore to the Calendar

YOUR NAME, being duly sworn deposes and says:

Chapter 2: Acting As Your Own Lawyer

1. I am the party named as defendant in the above-entitled action, and I am submitting this affidavit in support of the application to vacate the order herein dated July 18, 2005. I make this affidavit in support of this application for an order opening the default of the defendant and vacating and setting aside the default judgment entered against the defendant.

2. Upon information and belief, this action was commenced by affixing a copy of the summons and complaint on the outer of two lobby doors of the building wherein Deponent's apartment is located, together with at least five (5) other apartments and approximately twelve (12) other occupants. Note that the subject summons was allegedly placed where retail store flyers and other communications intended for any of the approximately twelve (12) occupants of YOUR Home Address are placed. Also, note that YOUR Home Address is a five (5) family dwelling, secured by two (2) security (lobby) doors.

3. Moreover, retired members of the Deponent's family also reside at the same apartment, and at all times, there was a working doorbell with an exterior button conspicuously labeled "3B." Nevertheless, Deponent is not aware of a single attempt to serve him personally.

Chapter 2: Acting As Your Own Lawyer

4. Plaintiff further alleges service by mailing a copy of the summons and complaint via United States Postal Service. However, the Deponent did not receive the aforesaid summons and complaint, and the Deponent's first notice of legal action was a Restraining Notice on his bank account and a Notice of Garnishment from his employer. As such, Plaintiff has failed to satisfy the four-prong service requirement of CPLR § 308(4). Specifically, 1. Impossibility of CPLR § 308(1) and CPLR § 308(2) with due diligence, 2. Affixing the summons to the dwelling place of usual abode, 3. Mailing summons to the last known residence of the deponent, and 4. Filing proof of service with the clerk of the court within twenty days of the affixing or mailing.

5. Despite having knowledge of Deponent's current work telephone number, from which Plaintiff could easily ascertain the physical location of Deponent's place of employment, Plaintiff never made a single attempt to find plaintiff's place of employment, thereby failing to exercise the requisite due diligence required to satisfy the service requirement of CPLR § 308(4). "There is substantial authority for the proposition that three attempts at residential service do not satisfy the 'due diligence' requirement where the process-server made no attempt to serve the defendant at his actual place of business, in particular where the

Chapter 2: Acting As Your Own Lawyer

place of business was known." *Sartor v. Toussaint*, 70 Fed. Appx. 11, 14 (2d Cir. 2002).

6. Additionally, "It is well settled that service pursuant to CPLR § 308(4) may only be used in those instances where service under CPLR § 308(1) and (2) cannot be made with due diligence." *Gurevitch v. Goodman*, 269 A.D.2d 355 (2000).

7. The Deponent did not appear and answer in this action and on July 18, 2005, judgment by default was entered against the Deponent in the amount of $5,110.75.

8. The deponent's failure to appear and consequently, his default, resulted from the fact that the Deponent never received notice of this action in time to defend.

9. Regarding the alleged mailed copy of the summons, it should be noted that, "There is no presumption at all, absent proof of mailing in an envelope properly addressed and stamped. *Uni-Serv Corp. v. Frede*, 271 N.Y.S.2d 478, 481 (N.Y. Civ. Ct. 1966) aff'd, 279 N.Y.S.2d 510 (N.Y. App. Term 1967).

10. As evident by the income execution in favor of Plaintiff (a copy is annexed hereto as Exhibit "A"), Plaintiff knew the location of Deponent's

Chapter 2: Acting As Your Own Lawyer

home and place of employment through the business dealings between them, yet never attempted to serve Deponent personally at his home or place of employment.

11. While the Deponent admits indebtedness to plaintiff, he denies the debt in the amount claimed. The excessive portion of the debt disputed herein represents a significant part of plaintiff's claim.

12. The aforementioned assertion is evident by a demand letter from plaintiff, wherein Plaintiff demanded an already inflated $3,583.59 from Deponent as the full amount of the debt due Plaintiff (a copy is annexed hereto as Exhibit "B"). Note that the subject account is the only account Deponent ever had with plaintiff.

13. Deponent asserts that the amount claimed by Plaintiff violates the Fair Debt Collection Practices Act, 15 USCS § 1692f(1) and CLPR 5001.

14. Further, Deponent made good faith efforts to resolve this matter during its inception, but Plaintiff insisted on charging Deponent unreasonable and excessive interest and fees and refused to settle the matter amicably.

Chapter 2: Acting As Your Own Lawyer

15. Instead, Plaintiff insisted on allowing the excessive interest and fees to accumulate and continued to harass Deponent despite Deponent's adamant refusal to pay the unfair interest and fees.

16. For this reason, Deponent asserts that Plaintiff failed to mitigate their damages and, therefore, "… cannot get judgment for the amount of this avoidable and unnecessary increase." Restatement, Contracts, § 336, subd [1], *Manufacturers & Traders Trust Co. v. Holley*, 438 N.Y.S.2d. 676, 688 (N.Y. City Ct. 1981). Moreover, in *Cohen v. Banks*, 642 N.Y.S.2d 797, 802 (1996), the Court ruled that the Plaintiff could not recover for injuries she might have reasonably avoided by timely prudent action because of the Plaintiff's "determination to maximize them (damages) rather than seeking legal relief."

17. A significant portion of plaintiff's alleged "damages" are self-incurred, and "self-incurred damages are not recoverable under the doctrine of avoidable consequences." *Jenkins v. Graham*, 237 So..2d 330, 332 (Fla. Dist. Ct. App. 1970).

18. Keeping in mind that Deponent is under no obligation to, and "need not conclusively establish the validity" of his position, it is clear from the facts of this case as established by the above, the showing of a meritorious defense; that the default

Chapter 2: Acting As Your Own Lawyer

judgment must be vacated, in the interests of justice. *Davis*, 713 F.2d 907, 916 (2d. Cir. 1983).

19. Deponent made one prior application on July 7, 2006 for relief regarding this index number. However, Deponent was unable to appear on July 21, 2006 at 9:30 AM, in time to defend same, because of a family health emergency, which the effects of the heat wave beginning on July 17th, and subsequent storm further complicated and compounded by creating power and water problems at Deponent's residence. As consequence, Deponent defaulted.

CONCLUSION

It is respectfully requested that this Court grant defendant's motion for an order opening the default of the defendant in this action, vacating and setting aside the judgment by default against the defendant entered on the 18th day of July, 2005; allowing the defendant to serve an answer herein or move in regard to the complaint within 30 days after service of a copy of the order granting defendant's motion with notice of entry and for such other and further relief as this Court deems just and proper.

Chapter 2: Acting As Your Own Lawyer

> Keep in mind that the time you have to vacate a default judgment varies from state to state; however, it is generally around one year. You should always contact your local court to verify.

> **The foregoing Affidavit accompanies the shorter Order to Show Cause.** Go to www.debtorselfhelp.com for editable versions of both documents.

Chapter 3: Statutes of Limitations

After completing this chapter, you will:

- ✓ Understand what statutes of limitation are
- ✓ Know how to handle expired debts

Statutes of Limitations

Laws that limit the time, ranging from three to 15 years, during which a plaintiff may sue a defendant for a debt or damages are called statutes of limitations.

Statutes of limitations vary from state to state. If the statute of limitations has expired for a debt, you could revive the debt and restart the clock by making a payment on the debt. For example, in New York, the statute of limitations is 6 years; therefore, if you have a debt older than six (6) years in New York, a debt collector no longer has the option to sue you. However, if you make a payment, the debt collector may have the option to sue you for that debt.

Glossary of Terms

affidavit: a sworn statement.

caselaw or **case law**: law created by decisions in earlier court cases, which lower courts within a given jurisdiction must follow.

citation: a reference to caselaw which a lower court in the same jurisdiction must follow, and other courts often find persuasive. We also use citations to refer to statutes (laws) or other legal authorities. Example of case citation: *Cavallaro v. The Law Office of Shapiro & Krcsiman*, 933 F. Supp. 1148, 1153 (E.D.N.Y. 1996)

complaint: the documents filed with a court by a plaintiff to initiate a lawsuit against a defendant

counterclaim: a claim against an adversary who made an original claim.

debt collector: anyone who regularly collects or attempts to collect debts owed or allegedly owed to another, but **does not include the original creditor**.

Glossary of Terms

default judgment: a decision entered against a plaintiff or defendant who does not appear in court to defend against a claim.

dunning letter or **demand letter**: a letter demanding payment for an alleged debt.

motion: a written or oral request to a court to make a decision (legal ruling).

pleadings: documents filed with a court.

pro se (also **pro per**): anyone who represents him/herself without the assistance of a lawyer.

shepardize: to determine whether case law is still current.

statutes of limitations: laws that limit the time, ranging from 3 to 15 years, during which a plaintiff may sue a defendant for a debt or damages.

validation notice: statement notifying you that you have thirty days to dispute a debt.

Recommended Legal Resources

www.debtorselfhelp.com: Debtor Self-Help is the companion resource for this book. Use Debtor Self-Help for ready-to-use legal documents that we especially tailored for debtors. Use the promotional code **BOOK1** to receive 50% off our Premium Debtors' Self-Help Package.
You can also use our forum to receive help from knowledgeable consumers who are similarly situated.

http://lp.findlaw.com/: Use FindLaw to locate additional on-point cases to support your arguments. Click on "Cases and Codes."

http://findacase.com/: FindACase is an excellent paid legal research service.

Scan QR Code

Table of Cases

Allen ex rel. Martin v. LaSalle Bank, N.A., 629 F.3d 364, 368 (3d Cir.2011); *LeBlanc v. Unifund CCR Partners*, 601 F.3d 1185, 1190 (11th Cir.2010); *Donohue*, 592 F.3d at 1030; *Ellis v. Solomon & Solomon, P.C.*, 591 F.3d 130, 135 (2d Cir.2010); *Ruth v. Triumph P'ships*, 577 F.3d 790, 805 (7th Cir.2009): The FDCPA "imposes liability without proof of an intentional violation."

Beattie v. D.M. Collections, Inc., 754 F.Supp. 383, 393 (D.Del.1991): "The threatening of a lawsuit which the debt collector knows or should know is unavailable or unwinnable by reason of a legal bar such as the statute of limitations is the kind of abusive practice the FDCPA was intended to eliminate."

Campuzano–Burgos v. Midland Credit Mgmt., Inc., 550 F.3d 294, 298 (3d Cir.2008): "A communication is deceptive for purposes of the Act if it can be reasonably read to have two or more different meanings, one of which is inaccurate."

Clomon v. Jackson, 988 F.2d 1314, 1318 (2d Cir.1993): A single violation of the FDCPA is enough to impose liability.

Table of Cases

Ellis v. Solomon & Solomon, P. C., 591 F.3d 130, 135 (2d Cir.2010): "…to recover damages under the FDCPA, a consumer does not need to show intentional conduct on the part of the debt collector."

English v. Gen. Elec. Co., 496 U.S. 72, 79–80 (1990): The FDCPA does not preempt consistent state laws, even when the state laws provide greater protection.

Kimber v. Fed. Fin. Corp., 668 F.Supp. 1480, 1487 (M.D.Ala.1987): "(A) debt collector's filing of a lawsuit on a debt that appears to be time-barred, without the debt collector having first determined after a reasonable inquiry that that limitations period has been or should be tolled, is an unfair and unconscionable means of collecting the debt."

Larsen v. JBC Legal Grp., P.C., 533 F.Supp.2d 290, 302–03 (E.D.N.Y.2008): Threatening legal action on time-barred debts violates the FDCPA.

LeBlanc v. Unifund CCR Partners, 601 F.3d 1185, 1190 (11th Cir.2010); *Donohue v. Quick Collect, Inc.*, 592 F.3d 1027, 1030 (9th Cir.2010); *Ruth v. Triumph P'ships*, 577 F.3d 790, 805 (7th Cir.2009): The FDCPA is generally characterized as a strict liability statute.

Table of Cases

Manufacturers & Traders Trust Co. v. Holley, 438 N.Y.S.2d. 676, 688 (N.Y. City Ct. 1981): Plaintiff failed to mitigate their damages and therefore, "…cannot get judgment for the amount of this avoidable and unnecessary increase."

Mendus v. Morgan & Associates, P.C., 994 P.2d 83, 88 (Okla.Civ.App.1999): Legal action constitutes an "initial communication" within the meaning of the FDCPA.

> Use cases from your circuit (states within your jurisdiction) whenever possible.

Judicial Divisions of the U.S.

The court system in the United States (and its territories) is geographically divided into judicial divisions called circuits. The circuit courts (also called courts of appeals) within the 13 circuits review decisions from lower courts in the same circuit. **The circuit courts in a given judicial division are the highest courts in that geographical area.**

The charts below show the states within each circuit:

1st Circuit
- Maine
- Massachusetts
- New Hampshire
- Puerto Rico
- Rhode Island

2nd Circuit
- Connecticut
- New York
- Vermont

3rd Circuit
- Delaware
- New Jersey
- Pennsylvania
- U.S. Virgin Islands

The Debtor's Self-Help Guide

Judicial Divisions of the U.S.

4th Circuit
- Maryland
- North Carolina
- South Carolina
- Virginia
- West Virginia

5th Circuit
- Louisiana
- Mississippi
- Texas

6th Circuit
- Kentucky
- Michigan
- Ohio
- Tennessee

7th Circuit
- Illinois
- Indiana
- Wisconsin

Judicial Divisions of the U.S.

8th Circuit
- Arkansas
- Iowa
- Minnesota
- Missouri
- Nebraska
- North Dakota
- South Dakota

9th Circuit
- Alaska
- Arizona
- California
- Guam
- Hawaii
- Idaho
- Montana
- Nevada
- Northern Mariana Islands
- Oregon
- Washington

Judicial Divisions of the U.S.

10th Circuit
- Colorado
- Kansas
- New Mexico
- Oklahoma
- Utah
- Wyoming

11th Circuit
- Alabama
- Florida
- Georgia

In addition to the abovementioned circuits, there are also the DC Circuit and the Federal Circuit. The DC Circuit and the Federal Circuit are federal appellate courts.

For our purposes, it is important to note that all judges in a given circuit (appellate jurisdiction) must follow case law from higher courts in that circuit.

Judicial Divisions of the U.S.

Let us examine a citation to determine which circuit issued the decision.

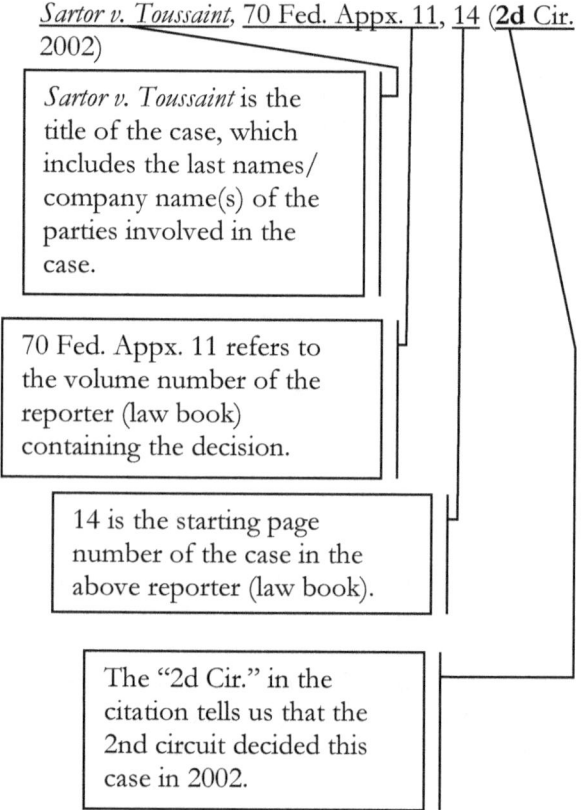

Sartor v. Toussaint, 70 Fed. Appx. 11, 14 (**2d** Cir. 2002)

Sartor v. Toussaint is the title of the case, which includes the last names/company name(s) of the parties involved in the case.

70 Fed. Appx. 11 refers to the volume number of the reporter (law book) containing the decision.

14 is the starting page number of the case in the above reporter (law book).

The "2d Cir." in the citation tells us that the 2nd circuit decided this case in 2002.

Citations without a number and a letter(s) in parenthesis plainly abbreviate the states that decided the cases.

www.ingramcontent.com/pod-product-compliance
Lightning Source LLC
Chambersburg PA
CBHW072245170526
45158CB00003BA/1012